Clothes
From
Many Lands

Acknowledgments

Executive Editor: Diane Sharpe
Supervising Editor: Stephanie Muller
Design Manager: Sharon Golden
Page Design: Ian Winton
Photography: Bryan and Cherry Alexander Photography: page 13; The Hutchison Library: pages 15, 17; Christine Osborne: page 25; Spectrum: page 27; Frank Spooner Pictures: page 21; Tony Stone International: cover (all), pages 7, 9, 19, 23; TRIP: page 11.

Library of Congress Cataloging-in-Publication Data

Jackson, Mike, 1946-
    Clothes from many lands/Mike Jackson; illustrated by John Bennett.
      p.   cm. — (Read all about it)
    Includes index.
    ISBN 0-8114-5726-5 Hardcover
    ISBN 0-8114-3738-8 Softcover
    1. Children's clothing — Juvenile literature. 2. Children — Costume — Juvenile literature. [1. Clothing and dress. 2. Costume.] I. Bennett, John, ill. II. Title. III. Series: Read all about it (Austin, Tex.)
TT635.J33 1995
391'.3—dc20

94-29421
CIP
AC

1 2 3 4 5 6 7 8 9 0 PO 00 99 98 97 96 95 94

Clothes
From
Many Lands

Mike Jackson

Illustrated by
John Bennett

STECK-VAUGHN
COMPANY
ELEMENTARY · SECONDARY · ADULT · LIBRARY

Many children wear clothes like these. But there are also many children who dress in a different way.

These boys
live in Peru.

I wear a hat to
shade my face
from the sun.

My hat helps
keep me warm in
the winter, too.

8

It's sunny in Peru, but it can also be very cold.

These girls live in Malaysia.

Sometimes we wear sarongs.

10

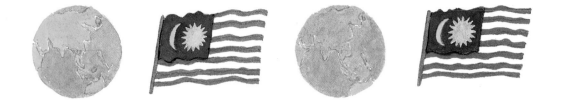

Sarongs feel cool when the weather is hot and damp.

These are Inuit
boys. They live
in northern Canada.

I like my thick clothes.
They keep me warm.

In northern Canada, many people wear clothes made from fur.

13

These two girls
live in Kenya,
which is in Africa.

These beads are very colorful.

All over the world, people have clothes for parties and other special occasions.

This girl lives
in Pakistan.

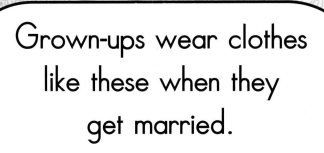

18

In many countries, people wear special clothes for weddings.

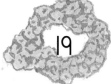

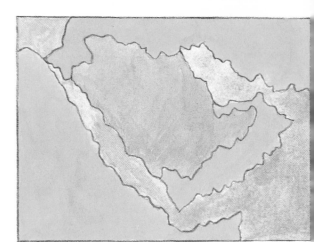

These boys live
in the desert of
Saudi Arabia.

My kaffiyeh keeps
the sun and sand
out of my face.

The sun is very hot in the desert, and strong winds blow the sand everywhere.

This girl is from Bali, which is in Indonesia.

I wear these beautiful clothes when I dance.

22

The dancing in Bali is famous all around the world.

These girls
live in India.

My sari is beautiful.
It is made from silk.

Much fabric is needed to make saris.

These Native
American boys
live in the southwestern
United States.

We like wearing
our buckskins
on special days.

Some Native Americans wear clothes like these for meetings called powwows.

29

These children come from different countries all around the world. Do you remember where each one lives?

Index